Comets

by Libby Romero

Table of Contents

Introduction	2
Chapter 1 What Is a Comet?	4
Chapter 2 How Did People Learn About Comets?	10
Chapter 3 Who Taught People About Comets?	14
Summary	20
Glossary	22
Index	24

Introduction

Comets are part of the **universe**. Comets look like bright stars. Comets have long tails. People know much about comets today.

▲ The universe has comets.

▲ Comets have tails.

Words to Know

astronomers

coma

comets

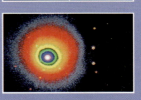
nucleus

orbit

scientists

telescopes

universe

See the Glossary on page 22.

Chapter 1

What Is a Comet?

A comet is a bright object in space. Comets are part of the universe.

▲ A comet is a bright object in space.

All comets have three main parts. One part is solid. The **nucleus** is the solid part.

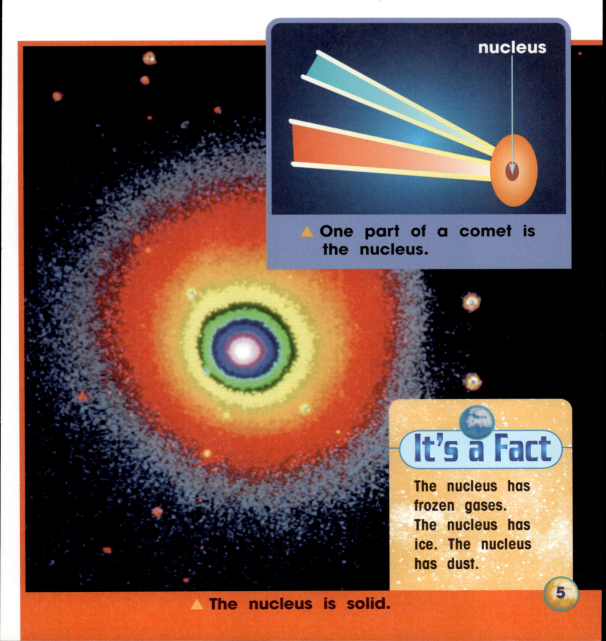

▲ One part of a comet is the nucleus.

It's a Fact

The nucleus has frozen gases. The nucleus has ice. The nucleus has dust.

▲ The nucleus is solid.

Chapter 1

The **coma** is part of a comet. The coma is dust. The coma is gases, too. The coma is around the nucleus.

Did You Know?

The comas of comets are very large. Some comas are bigger than the sun.

▲ This comet has a bright coma.

What Is a Comet?

The tail is another part of a comet. The tail has dust. The tail has gases, too.

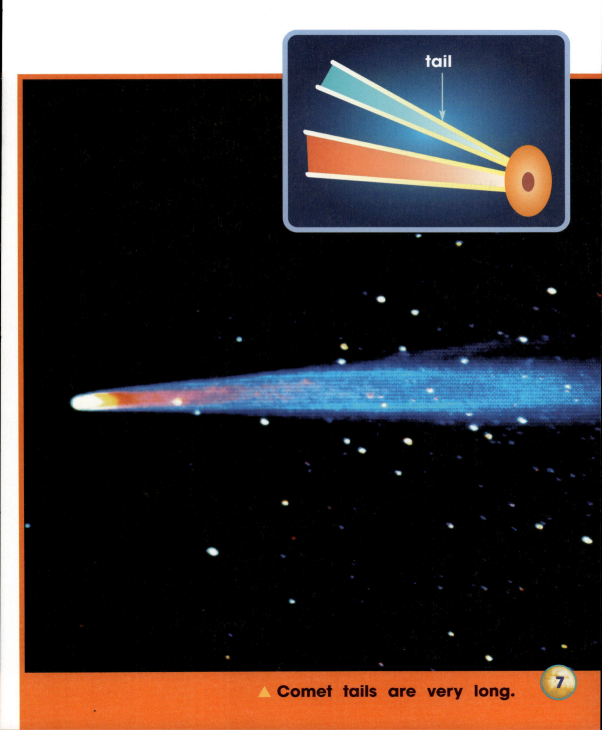

▲ Comet tails are very long.

Chapter 1

The dust in comets is very old. The rocks in comets are very old.

Picture This

Look at the rock from a comet. Pretend the rock is in your hand. How does the rock feel?

▲ Parts of comets are very old.

What Is a Comet?

Scientists still have questions about comets. Scientists want to know more. Scientists want to know where comets begin.

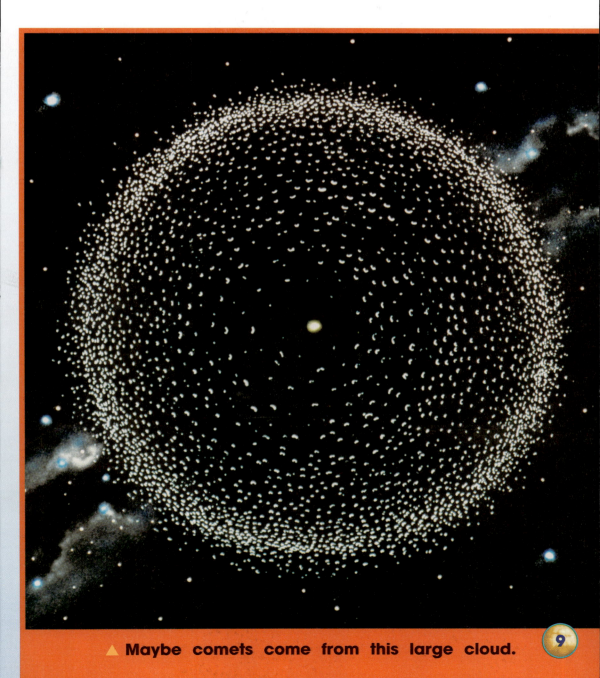

▲ Maybe comets come from this large cloud.

Chapter 2

How Did People Learn About Comets?

People watched the sky. People saw comets. People learned about comets.

It's a Fact

Long ago people were scared of comets. People thought comets made bad things happen.

▲ People learned by watching the sky.

Astronomers watched comets. Astronomers wrote about comets. Chinese astronomers wrote about comets. People wrote each time a comet appeared.

It's a Fact

Chinese astronomers helped other astronomers learn about comets.

▲ This drawing tells about when a comet appeared.

Chapter 2

People cannot see most comets from Earth. Early astronomers saw only bright comets. Astronomers needed better tools to see other comets.

▲ Early astronomers had few tools to study comets.

How Did People Learn About Comets?

Astronomers had **telescopes** by the 17th century. Then, astronomers saw far into space. Astronomers saw more comets.

Did You Know?

Astronomers wrote about more than 2,000 comets. People see many comets with telescopes.

▲ Astronomers saw comets through telescopes.

Chapter 3

Who Taught People About Comets?

Many astronomers taught people about comets. Astronomers studied comets long ago.

▲ Astronomers taught people about comets.

Tycho Brahe was an astronomer. Brahe watched a bright comet for many months. Brahe wrote about the comet. He proved comets were part of the universe.

▲ Tycho Brahe

▲ Comets are part of the universe.

Chapter 3

Sir Isaac Newton used a telescope. Newton watched how comets move in the universe. Newton proved that comets **orbit** the sun. Newton proved that comets move around the sun.

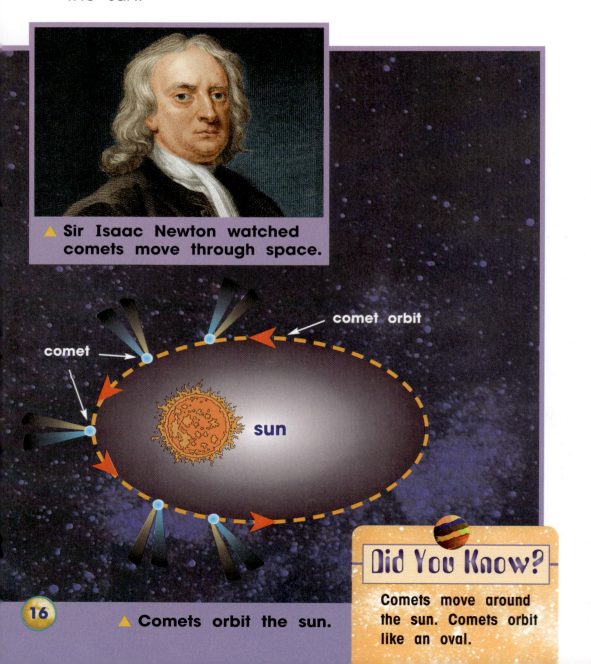

▲ Sir Isaac Newton watched comets move through space.

▲ Comets orbit the sun.

Did You Know?

Comets move around the sun. Comets orbit like an oval.

Who Taught People About Comets?

Edmond Halley proved that comets come back. Halley studied comets. One comet came back every 76 years. Halley told people when to look for the comet.

Solve This

A comet last appeared in 1986. This comet comes back every 76 years. When will the comet come back?

Answer: 2062

▲ Halley wrote about this comet.

▲ Edmond Halley proved that comets come back.

Chapter 3

Modern scientists study comets. Scientists use many new things to study comets. Scientists have very large telescopes.

▲ Scientists see comets through telescopes.

Who Taught People About Comets?

Scientists want to learn about comets. Scientists send machines to comets. Scientists study materials from comets. Scientists hope to learn more about the universe.

▲ This machine collected dust from a comet.

Summary

Comets are part of the universe. People watched comets. Astronomers taught people about comets long ago. Astronomers still study comets today.

Comets

What Is a Comet?

- bright object in space
- part of the universe
- three main parts
  - nucleus
  - coma
  - tail
- very old

How Did People Learn About Comets?

- watched the sky
- watched comets
- wrote about comets
- used telescopes

Who Taught People About Comets?

- astronomers
- Tycho Brahe
- Sir Isaac Newton
- Edmond Halley
- modern scientists

Think About It

1. What is a comet?
2. How did people learn about comets?
3. Why do scientists send machines to comets?

Glossary

astronomers people who study the universe

Early **astronomers** saw only bright comets.

coma dust and gases around the nucleus

The **coma** is part of a comet.

comets bright objects in space

Comets are part of the universe.

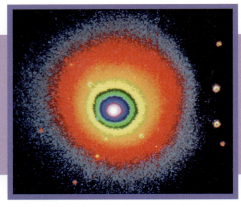

nucleus the middle of an object

The **nucleus** is the solid part.

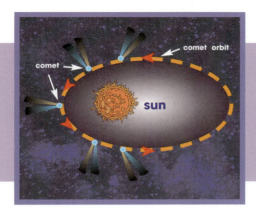

orbit move around another object in the universe

*Newton proved that comets **orbit** the sun.*

scientists people who study science

*Modern **scientists** study comets.*

telescopes tools used to study outer space

*Astronomers had **telescopes** by the 17th century.*

universe everything in space

*Comets are part of the **universe**.*

Index

astronomers, 11–15, 20

Brahe, Tycho, 15

Chinese, 11

coma, 6

comets, 2, 4–20

Halley, Edmond, 17

Newton, Sir Isaac, 16

nucleus, 5–6

old, 8

orbit, 16

scientists, 9, 18–19

tail, 2, 7

telescopes, 13, 16, 18

tools, 12

universe, 2, 4, 15–16, 19–20